The 5 Pillars of Self-Discipline

The 5 Pillars of
Self-Discipline

Steve Pavlina

WAKING LION PRESS

ISBN 978-1-4341-0566-0

Published by Waking Lion Press, an imprint of the Editorium

Waking Lion Press™ and Editorium™ are trademarks of:

The Editorium, LLC
West Jordan, UT 84081-6132
www.editorium.com

The views expressed in this book are the responsibility of the author and do not necessarily represent the position of Waking Lion Press. The reader alone is responsible for the use of any ideas or information provided by this book.

Contents

1	Self-Discipline	1
2	Acceptance	8
3	Willpower	17
4	Hard Work	25
5	Industry	32
6	Persistence	40

Chapter 1

Self-Discipline

In this book I'll be focusing on what I call the *five pillars of self-discipline*.

The Five Pillars of Self-Discipline

The five pillars of self-discipline are: Acceptance, Willpower, Hard Work, Industry, and Persistence. If you take the first letter of each word, you get the acronym "A WHIP" — a convenient way to remember them, since many people associate self-discipline with whipping themselves into shape.

In each chapter, I'll explore one of these pillars, explaining why it's important and how to develop it. But first a general overview. . . .

What Is Self-Discipline?

Self-discipline is the ability to get yourself to take action regardless of your emotional state.

Imagine what you could accomplish if you could simply get yourself to follow through on your best intentions no matter what. Picture yourself saying to your body, "You're overweight. Lose 20 pounds." Without self-discipline that intention won't become manifest. But with sufficient self-discipline, it's a done deal. The pinnacle of self-discipline is when you reach the point that when you make a conscious decision, it's virtually guaranteed you'll follow through on it.

Self-discipline is one of many personal development tools available to you. Of course it is not a panacea. Nevertheless, the problems which self-discipline can solve are important, and while there are other ways to solve these problems, self-discipline absolutely shreds them. Self-discipline can empower you to overcome any addiction or lose any amount of weight. It can wipe out procrastination, disorder, and ignorance. Within the domain of problems it can solve, self-discipline is simply unmatched. Moreover, it becomes a powerful teammate when combined with other tools like passion, goal-setting, and planning.

Building Self-Discipline

My philosophy of how to build self-discipline is best explained by an analogy. Self-discipline is like a muscle. The more you train it, the stronger you become. The less you train it, the weaker you become.

Just as everyone has different muscular strength, we all possess different levels of self-discipline. Everyone has some — if you can hold your breath a few seconds, you have some self-discipline. But not everyone has developed their discipline to the same degree.

Just as it takes muscle to build muscle, it takes self-discipline to build self-discipline.

The way to build self-discipline is analogous to using progressive weight training to build muscle. This means lifting weights that are close to your limit. Note that when you weight train, you lift weights that are within your ability to lift. You push your muscles until they fail, and then you rest.

Similarly, the basic method to build self-discipline is

to tackle challenges that you can successfully accomplish but which are near your limit. This doesn't mean trying something and failing at it every day, nor does it mean staying within your comfort zone. You will gain no strength trying to lift a weight that you cannot budge, nor will you gain strength lifting weights that are too light for you. You must start with weights/challenges that are within your current ability to lift but which are near your limit.

Progressive training means that once you succeed, you increase the challenge. If you keep working out with the same weights, you won't get any stronger. Similarly, if you fail to challenge yourself in life, you won't gain any more self-discipline.

Just as most people have very weak muscles compared to how strong they could become with training, most people are very weak in their level of self-discipline.

It's a mistake to try to push yourself too hard when trying to build self-discipline. If you try to transform your entire life overnight by setting dozens of new goals for yourself and expecting yourself to follow through consistently starting the very next day, you're almost certain to fail. This is like a person going to the gym for the first time ever and packing 300 pounds on the bench press. You will only look silly.

If you can only lift 10 lbs, you can only lift 10 lbs. There's no shame in starting where you are. I recall when I began working with a personal trainer several years ago, on my first attempt at doing a barbell shoulder press, I could only lift a 7-lb bar with no weight on it. My shoulders were very weak because I'd never trained them. But within a few months I was up to 60 lbs.

Similarly, if you're very undisciplined right now, you can still use what little discipline you have to build more. The more disciplined you become, the easier life gets. Challenges that were once impossible for you will eventually seem like child's play. As you get stronger, the same weights will seem lighter and lighter.

Don't compare yourself to other people. It won't help. You'll only find what you expect to find. If you think you're weak, everyone else will seem stronger. If you think you're strong, everyone else will seem weaker. There's no point in doing this. Simply look at where you are now, and aim to get better as you go forward.

Let's consider an example.

Suppose you want to develop the ability to do 8 solid hours of work each day, since you know it will make a real difference in your career. I was listening to an audio program this morning that quoted a study saying the average office worker spends 37% of their time in idle socializing, not to mention other vices that chew up more than 50% of work time with unproductive non-work. So there's plenty of room for improvement.

Perhaps you try to work a solid 8-hour day without succumbing to distractions, and you can only do it once. The next day you fail utterly. That's OK. You did one rep of 8 hours. Two is too much for you. So cut back a bit. What duration would allow you to successfully do 5 reps (i.e. a whole week)? Could you work with concentration for one hour a day, five days in a row? If you can't do that, cut back to 30 minutes or whatever you can do. If you succeed (or if you feel that would be too easy), then increase the challenge (i.e. the resistance).

Once you've mastered a week at one level, take it up a notch the next week. And continue with this progressive training until you've reached your goal.

While analogies like this are never perfect, I've gotten a lot of mileage out of this one. By raising the bar just a little each week, you stay within your capabilities and grow stronger over time. But when doing weight training, the actual work you do doesn't mean anything. There's no intrinsic benefit in lifting a weight up and down — the benefit comes from the muscle growth.

However, when building self-discipline, you also get the benefit of the work you've done along the way, so that's even better. It's great when your training produces something of value *and* makes you stronger.

Throughout this book we'll dive more deeply into the five pillars of self-discipline.

Chapter 2

Acceptance

The first of the five pillars of self-discipline is acceptance. Acceptance means that you perceive reality accurately and consciously acknowledge what you perceive.

This may sound simple and obvious, but in practice it's extremely difficult. If you experience chronic difficulties in a particular area of your life, there's a strong chance that the root of the problem is a failure to accept reality as it is.

Why is acceptance a pillar of self-discipline? The most basic mistake people make with respect to self-discipline is a failure to accurately perceive and accept their present situation. Remember the analogy between self-discipline and weight training? If you're going to succeed at weight training, the first step is to figure out what weights you can already lift. How strong are you right now? Until you figure out where you stand right now, you cannot adopt a sensible training program.

If you haven't consciously acknowledged where you stand right now in terms of your level of self-discipline, it's highly unlikely that you're going to improve at all in this area. Imagine a would-be bodybuilder who has no idea how much weight s/he can lift and arbitrarily adopts a training routine. It's virtually certain that the chosen weights will be either too heavy or too light. If the weights are too heavy, the trainee won't be able to lift them at all and thus will experience no muscle growth. And if the weights are too light, the trainee will lift them easily but won't build any muscle in doing so.

Similarly, if you want to increase your self-discipline, you must know where you stand right now. How strong is your discipline at this moment? Which challenges are easy for you, and which are virtually impossible for you?

Here's a list of challenges to get you thinking about where you stand right now (in no particular order):

- Do you shower/bathe every day?

- Do you get up at the same time every morning? Including weekends?

- Are you overweight?
- Do you have any addictions (caffeine, nicotine, sugar, etc.) you'd like to break but haven't?
- Is your email inbox empty right now?
- Is your office neat and well organized?
- Is your home neat and well organized?
- How much time do you waste in a typical day? On a weekend?
- If you make a promise to someone, what's the percentage chance you'll keep it?
- If you make a promise to yourself, what's the percentage chance you'll keep it?
- Could you fast for one day?
- How well organized is your computer's hard drive?
- How often do you exercise?
- What's the greatest physical challenge you've ever faced, and how long ago was it?

Acceptance

- How many hours of focused work do you complete in a typical workday?

- How many items on your to do list are older than 90 days?

- Do you have clear, written goals? Do you have written plans to achieve them?

- If you lost your job, how much time would you spend each day looking for a new one, and how long would you maintain that level of effort?

- How much TV do you currently watch? Could you give up TV for 30 days?

- How do you look right now? What does your appearance say about your level of discipline (clothes, grooming, etc)?

- Do you primarily select foods to eat based on health considerations or on taste/satiety?

- When was the last time you consciously adopted a positive new habit? Discontinued a bad habit?

- Are you in debt? Do you consider this debt an investment or a mistake?

- Did you decide in advance to be reading this blog right now, or did it just happen?
- Can you tell me what you'll be doing tomorrow? Next weekend?
- On a scale of 1–10, how would you rate your overall level of self-discipline?
- What more could you accomplish if you could answer that last question with a 9 or 10?
- Just as there are different muscle groups which you train with different exercises, there are different areas of self-discipline: disciplined sleep, disciplined diet, disciplined work habits, disciplined communication, etc. It takes different exercises to build discipline in each area.

My advice is to identify an area where your discipline is weakest, assess where you stand right now, acknowledge and accept your starting point, and design a training program for yourself to improve in this area. Start out with some easy exercises you know you can do, and gradually progress to greater challenges.

Progressive training works with self-discipline just as it does with building muscle. For example, if you

Acceptance

can barely get out of bed at 10AM, are you likely to succeed at waking up at 5AM every morning? Probably not. But could you master getting up at 9:45AM? Very likely. And once you've done that, could you progress to 9:30 or 9:15? Sure. When I started getting up at 5AM consistently, I had already done it several times for a few days in a row, and my normal wake-up time was 6–6:30 AM, so that next step was challenging but achievable for me partly because I was already within range of it.

Without acceptance you get either ignorance or denial. With ignorance you simply don't know how disciplined you are — you've probably never even thought about it. You don't know that you don't know. You'll only have a fuzzy notion of what you can and can't do. You'll experience some easy successes and some dismal failures, but you're more likely to blame the task or blame yourself instead of simply acknowledging that the "weight" was too heavy for you and that you need to become stronger.

When you're in a state of denial about your level of discipline, you're locked into a false view of reality. You're either overly pessimistic or optimistic about your capabilities. And like the trainee who doesn't know his/her own strength, you won't get much better because it's unlikely you'll be able to hit the proper training zone by accident. On the pessimistic side, you'll only pick up easy weights and avoid the heavy ones which you could actually lift and which would make you stronger. And on the optimistic side, you'll keep trying to lift weights that are too heavy for you and failing, and afterwards you may either beat yourself up or resolve to try harder, neither of which will make you stronger.

I have personally reaped tremendous benefits from pursuing the path of self-discipline. When I was 20 years old, I lived in a small studio apartment, and my sleep hours were something like 4AM to 1pm. My diet included lots of fast food and junk food. I didn't exercise except for sometimes taking long walks. Getting the mail seemed like a significant accomplishment each day, and the highlight of my day was hanging out with friends. At the end of a month, I couldn't really think of many salient events that occurred during the month. I had no job, no car, no income, no goals, no plans, and no real future. All I felt I had was a lot of problems that weren't getting any better. I had no sense that I could control my path through life. I would simply wait for things to happen and then react to them.

But eventually I faced the reality that trying to wait out my life wasn't working. If I was going to get anywhere, I was going to have to do something about it.

Acceptance

And initially this meant tackling a lot of difficult challenges, but I overcame them and grew a lot stronger in a short period of time.

Fast forward fourteen years, and it's like night and day. I get up at 5 AM each morning. I exercise six days a week. I eat a purely vegan diet with lots of fresh vegetables. My home office is well organized. My physical inbox and my email inbox are both empty. I'm married with two kids and live in a nice house. A binder sits on my desk with my written goals and detailed plans to achieve them, and several of my 2005 goals have already been accomplished. I've never been more clear about what I wanted, and I'm doing what I love. I know I'm making a difference.

None of this just happened. It was intentional. And it certainly didn't happen overnight. It took a lot of years of hard work. It's still hard work, but I've become a lot stronger such that things that would have been insurmountable for me at age 20 are easy today, which means I can tackle bigger challenges and therefore achieve even better results. If I had tried to do everything I'm doing now when I was 20, I would have failed utterly. 20-year old Steve wouldn't have been able to handle it, not even for one day. But for 34-year old Steve, it's easy. And what's really exciting for me is to think of what

48-year old Steve will be able to accomplish . . . relative to my life path of course, not anyone else's.

I *am* telling you this to impress you, not with me but with yourself. I want you to be impressed by what you can accomplish over the next 5–10 years if you progressively build your self-discipline. It will not be easy, but it will be worth it. The first step is to openly accept where you are right now, whether you feel good about it or not. Surrender yourself to what you have to work with — maybe it isn't fair, but it is what it is. And you won't get any stronger until you accept where you are right now.

Chapter 3

Willpower

> The difference between a successful person and others is not a lack of strength, not a lack of knowledge, but rather a lack of will.
>
> *Vince Lombardi*

Willpower — such a dirty word these days. How many commercials have you seen that attempt to position their products as a substitute for willpower? They begin by telling you that willpower doesn't work and then attempt to sell you something "fast and easy" like a diet pill or some wacky exercise equipment. Often they'll even guarantee impossible results in a dramatically short period of time — that's a safe bet because people who lack willpower probably won't take the time to return these useless products.

But guess what . . . willpower does work. But in order to take full advantage of it, you must learn what it can and cannot do. People who say willpower doesn't work are trying to use it in a way that's beyond its capabilities.

What Is Willpower?

Willpower is your ability to set a course of action and say, "Engage!"

Willpower provides an intensely powerful yet temporary boost. Think of it as a one-shot thruster. It burns out quickly, but if directed intelligently, it can provide the burst you need to overcome inertia and create momentum.

Willpower is the spearhead of self-discipline. To use a World War II analogy, willpower would be D-Day, the Normandy Invasion. It was the gigantic battle that turned the tide of the war and got things moving in a new direction, even though it took another year to reach VE Day (Victory in Europe). To make that kind of effort every day of the war would have been impossible.

Willpower is a concentration of force. You gather up

all your energy and make a massive thrust forward. You attack your problems strategically at their weakest points until they crack, allowing you enough room to maneuver deeper into their territory and finish them off.

The application of willpower includes the following steps:

1. Choose your objective

2. Create a plan of attack

3. Execute the plan

With willpower you may take your time implementing steps 1 and 2, but when you get to step 3, you've got to hit it hard and fast.

Don't try to tackle your problems and challenges in such a way that a high level of willpower is required every day. Willpower is unsustainable. If you attempt to use it for too long, you'll burn out. It requires a level of energy that you can maintain only for a short period of time . . . in most cases the fuel is spent within a matter of days.

Use Willpower to Create Self-Sustaining Momentum

So if willpower can only be used in short, powerful bursts, then what's the best way to apply it? How do you keep from slipping back into old patterns once the temporary willpower blast is over?

The best way to use willpower is to establish a beachhead, such that further progress can be made with far less effort than is required of the initial thrust. Remember D-Day — once the Allies had established a beachhead, the road ahead was much easier for them. It was still challenging to be sure, especially with the close quarters fighting among hedge rows in France before the Rhino Tanks began plowing through them, but it was a lot easier than trying to maintain the focus, energy, and coordination of a full scale beach invasion every single day for another year.

So the proper use of willpower is to establish that beachhead — to permanently change the territory itself such that it's easier to continue moving on. Use willpower to reduce the ongoing need for such a high level of sustained force.

An Example

Let's put all of the above together into a concrete example.

Suppose your objective is to lose 20 pounds. You attempt to go on a diet. It takes willpower, and you do OK with it the first week. But within a few weeks you've fallen back into old habits and gained all the weight back. You try again with different diets, but the result is still the same. You can't sustain momentum for long enough to reach your goal weight.

That's to be expected though because willpower is temporary. It's for sprints, not marathons. Willpower requires conscious focus, and conscious focus is very draining — it cannot be maintained for long. Something will eventually distract you.

Here's how to tackle that same goal with the proper application of willpower. You accept that you can only apply a short burst of willpower . . . maybe a few days at best. After that it's gone. So you'd better use that willpower to alter the territory around you in such a way that maintaining momentum won't be as hard as building it in the first place. You need to use your willpower to establish a beachhead on the shores of your goal.

So you sit down and make a plan. This doesn't require

much energy, and you can spread the work out over many days.

You identify all the various targets you'll need to strike if you want to have a chance of success. First, all the junk food needs to leave your kitchen, including anything you have a tendency to overeat, and you need to replace it with foods that will help you lose weight, like fruits and veggies. Secondly, you know you'll be tempted to get fast food if you come home hungry and don't have anything ready to eat, so you decide to precook a week's worth of food in advance each weekend. That way you always have something in the refrigerator. You set aside a block of several hours each weekend to buy groceries and cook all your food for the week. Plus you get a decent cookbook of healthy recipes. Create a weight chart and post it on your bathroom wall. Get a decent scale that can measure weight and body fat% . Make a list of sample meals (5 breakfasts, 5 lunches, and 5 dinners), and post it on your refrigerator. And so on. . . . At this point all of this goes into the written plan.

Then you execute — hard and fast. You can probably implement the whole plan in one day. Attend your first Weight Watchers meeting and get all the materials. Purge the unhealthy food from the kitchen. Buy the new groceries, the new cookbook, and the new scale.

Post the weight chart and the sample meals list. Select recipes and cook a batch of food for the week. Whew!

By the end of the day, you've used your willpower not to diet directly but to establish the conditions that will make your diet easier to follow. When you wake up the next morning, you'll find your environment dramatically changed in accordance with your plan. Your fridge will be stocked with plenty of pre-cooked healthy food for you to eat. There won't be any junkie problem foods in your home. You'll be a member of Weight Watchers and will have weekly meetings to attend. You'll have a regular block of time set aside for grocery shopping and food prep. It will still require some discipline to follow your diet, but you've already changed things so much that it won't be nearly as difficult as it would be without these changes.

Here are some previous blog entries that will give you even more ideas for modifying your environment:

Environmental Reinforcement of Your Goals

https://stevepavlina.com/blog/2004/12/environmental-reinforcement-of-your-goals/

Are Your Friends an Elevator or a Cage?

https://stevepavlina.com/blog/2004/12/are-your-friends-an-elevator-or-a-cage/

Your Personal Accountability System

https://stevepavlina.com/blog/2005/02/your-personal-accountability-system/

Don't use willpower to attack your biggest problem directly. Use willpower to attack the environmental and social obstacles that perpetuate the problem. Establish a beachhead first, and then fortify your position (i.e. turn it into a habit, such as by doing a 30-Day Challenge):

https://stevepavlina.com/blog/2005/04/30-days-to-success/

Habit puts action on autopilot, such that very little willpower is required for ongoing progress, allowing you to practically coast towards your goal.

Chapter 4

Hard Work

The big secret in life is that there is no big secret. Whatever your goal, you can get there if you're willing to work.

Oprah Winfrey

Hard work — yet another dirty word.

Hard Work Defined

My definition of hard work is that which challenges you.

And why is challenge important? Why not just do what's easiest?

Most people will do what's easiest and avoid hard work — and that's precisely why you should do the opposite. The superficial opportunities of life will be attacked by hordes of people seeking what's easy. The much tougher challenges will usually see a lot less competition and a lot more opportunity.

There's an African gold mine two miles deep. It cost tens of millions of dollars to construct, but it's one of the most lucrative gold mines ever. These miners tackled a very challenging problem with a lot of hard work, but ultimately it's paying off.

I remember when I was developing the PC game Dweep in 1999, I spent four months full-time working to create a design doc that was only five pages long. It was a logic puzzle game, and I found it extremely challenging to get the design just right. After the design was done, everything else took only two more months — programming, artwork, music, sound effects, writing the installer, and launching the game.

I spent all this time intentionally working on design because at the time, I believed this was where I could get the competitive edge I needed. I knew I couldn't compete on the basis of the game's technical attributes. Before I started on the game, I surveyed the competition and found a lot of games that I considered "low hanging fruit." Most of the market was flooded with clones of older games, the kind of stuff that's easiest to make. And most of my early games were short on design as well, mostly aim-and-shoot arcade games.

It was much, much harder to design an original game with unique gameplay. But it paid off handsomely. Dweep won the Shareware Industry Award in 2000, and an improved version of the game (Dweep Gold) won that same award the following year. As a result of the success of that game, I was interviewed by a reporter for the *New York Times*, and my interview along with a nice photo appeared in the June 13, 2001 edition (business section). First released on June 1, 1999, Dweep is now beginning its 7th year of sales. It can't compete with today's technology. It couldn't compete on technology when it was first released. But it still competes well on design with the best of the other competitors in its field. I discovered there are a lot of players who prefer a well-designed game with dated graphics than a shallow light show with the latest technology. The long-term success of this game brought home the lesson that hard work does pay.

There's no way Dweep would have been able to hold out this long if I had taken the easy way out during the design phase. I dug for gold two miles deep, so it was much harder for anyone else to unseat the game from its position in the market. In order to do that, they'd have to outdig me, and very few people are willing to do that because creative game design is excruciatingly difficult. Everyone says they have a cool game idea, but to actually turn it into something workable, fun, and innovative is very hard work. When I look at other games that are successful over a period of 5+ years, I consistently see a willingness to take on hard work that others aren't willing to tackle. And yet today the market is even more overcrowded with cloned drivel than when I started.

Strong challenge is commonly connected with strong results. Sure you can get lucky every once in a while and find an easy path to success. But will you be able to maintain that success, or is it just a fluke? Will you be able to repeat it? Once other people learn how you did it, will you find yourself overloaded with competition?

When you discipline yourself to do what is hard, you

gain access to a realm of results that are denied everyone else. The willingness to do what is difficult is like having a key to a special private treasure room.

The nice thing about hard work is that it's universal. It doesn't matter what industry you're in — hard work can be used to achieve positive long-term results regardless of the specifics.

I'm using this same philosophy in building this personal development business. I do a lot of things that are hard. I try to address topics that other people don't and bypass the low hanging fruit. I strive to explore topics deeply and search for the gold. I do lots of reading and research. I write lengthy articles and give my best ideas away for free, so I'm constantly forced to better my best. I launched this business in October of last year and have been working on it full time for essentially no pay.

Meanwhile I'm working hard in Toastmasters to build my speaking skills (my one-year anniversary was June 2nd). I belong to two different clubs and attend 6–7 meetings per month. I became a club officer about a month after joining, and I was just elected to a second officer position. I've given many speeches, all of them for free. I've competed in every speech contest since I've joined. If I had put all this time into my games business, I'd have a lot more money right now. It's a lot of hard work, and I've probably got at least another year of training before I'm ready to go pro. But I'm willing to pay the price whatever it takes. I'm not going to take the easy path to a shallow position where I will only come crashing back down again. I won't get up on a stage and spout a bunch of fluffy self-help sound bites that still garner applause and a paycheck but which don't ultimately help anyone. If it takes years, it takes years.

I'm taking the same approach to writing my book. It's a lot of hard work. But I want this to be the kind of book that people will still be reading 10 years from now. Writing a book like this is at least 10x harder than the kinds of books I see dominating the psychology section of bookstores today. But most of those books will be off the shelves in a year, and few people will even remember them.

Hard work pays off. When someone tells you otherwise, beware the sales pitch for something "fast and easy" that's about to come next. The greater your capacity for hard work, the more rewards fall within your grasp. The deeper you can dig, the more treasure you can potentially find.

Being healthy is hard work. Finding and maintaining a successful relationship is hard work. Raising kids is hard work. Getting organized is hard work. Setting goals, making plans to achieve them, and staying on track is hard work. Even being happy is hard work (true happiness that comes from high self-esteem, not the fake kind that comes from denial and escapism).

Hard work goes hand-in-hand with acceptance. One of the things you must accept are those areas of your life that won't succumb to anything less than hard work. Perhaps you've had no luck finding a fulfilling relationship. Maybe the only way it's going to happen is if you accept you're going to have to do what you've been avoiding. Perhaps you want to lose weight. Maybe it's time to accept that the path to your goal requires disciplined diet and exercise (both hard work). Perhaps you want to increase your income. Maybe you should accept that the only way it will happen is with a lot of hard work.

Your life will reach a whole new level when you stop avoiding and fearing hard work and simply surrender to it. Make it your ally instead of your enemy. It's a potent tool to have on your side.

If you want to read another perspective on hard work, see *Hard Work:*

https://stevepavlina.com/blog/2005/03/hard-work/

Chapter 5

Industry

Industry is working hard. In contrast to hard work, being industrious doesn't necessarily mean doing work that's challenging or difficult. It simply means putting in the time. You can be industrious doing easy work or hard work.

Imagine you have a baby. You'll spend a lot of time changing diapers. But that isn't really hard work — it's just a matter of doing it over and over many times each day.

In life there are many tasks that aren't necessarily difficult, but they collectively require a significant time investment. If you don't discipline yourself to stay on top of them, they can make a big mess of your life. Just think of all the little things you need to do: shopping, cooking, cleaning, laundry, taxes, paying bills, home maintenance, childcare, etc. And this is just for home — if you include work the list grows even longer. These things may not reach your A-list for importance, but they still need to be done.

Self-discipline requires that you develop the capacity to put in the time where it's needed. A lot of messes are created when we refuse to put in the time to do what needs to be done — and to do it correctly. Such messes range from a messy desk or cluttered email inbox all the way down to an Enron or Worldcom. Big mess or small mess — take your pick. Either way a significant contributing factor is the refusal to do what needs to be done.

Sometimes it's clear what needs to be done. Sometimes it isn't clear at all. But ignoring the mess won't help no matter what. If you don't know what needs to be done, the first step is to figure it out. This may require you to seek out information and educate yourself. In order to launch this blog last year, I had to figure out how to do it. I took time to educate myself by reading other blogs and evaluating various blogging tools. It wasn't difficult for me, but it required a significant time investment.

Sometimes we allow little annoyances to linger a bit too long. In January my wife and I bought a new house. But it was only last weekend we finally unpacked the last box. We did most of the unpacking in the first few weeks after the move, but a couple boxes were shoved into a corner, and neither one of us wanted to unpack them. Why? We didn't know where to put the stuff they contained. It seemed simplest to just ignore the problem and hope the boxes would magically unpack themselves. Finally we got them unpacked last weekend and took care of a few other home repairs that had been on the back burner as well.

It wasn't difficult or costly to do these things. It was simply a matter of time to get them done. It didn't require much skill or brainpower. All we had to do was just accept that they needed to be done, take a few minutes to figure out how to do them, and then do them.

Put in the Time

There are many problems in life where the solution is largely a brainless time investment. If your email inbox is overloaded, this is not a challenging problem. Believe me — there are bigger challenges in life than handling old correspondence. I guarantee you have the brainpower to handle it. Getting your email inbox to empty is purely a matter of time. Maybe it will take you several hours to do it. If it's worth several hours to get it done, then put in the time. Maybe enjoy some relaxing music as you do. Otherwise just hit *Ctrl-A* followed by *Delete*, and be done with it.

How many problems do you have on your to do list right now that can be solved with the simple application of industry? Sometimes you don't need to be particularly creative or clever about it — a brute force solution will do. But it's easy to get stuck in a pattern of wishing that a brute force solution wasn't necessary. It's tedious. It's boring. It's not that important anyway. And yet it still needs to be done.

By all means if you can find a way to avoid a time-consuming solution and find a faster or better way to bypass or eliminate the problem, take advantage of it. Delegate it, delete it — do whatever you can to remove the time burden. But if you know it's something that won't get done except via your personal time investment, like the ornery boxes in my home that refused to self-unpack, then just accept it and get it off your plate. Don't complain. Don't whine. Just do it.

Develop Your Personal Productivity

Disciplining yourself to be industrious allows you to squeeze more value out of your time. Time is a constant, but your personal productivity is not. Some people will use the hours of their day far more efficiently than others. It's amazing that people will spend extra money to buy a faster computer or a fuel efficient car, but they'll barely pay any attention to their personal capacity. Your personal productivity will do a lot more for you than a computer or a car in the long run. Give an industrious programmer a 10-year old computer, and s/he'll get much more done with it over the course of a year than a lazy programmer with state of the art technology.

Despite all the technology and gadgets we have available that can potentially make us more efficient, your personal productivity is still your greatest bottleneck. Don't look to technology to make you more productive. If you don't consider yourself productive without technology, you won't be productive with it — it will only serve to mask your bad habits. But if you're already industrious without technology, it can help you become even more so. Think of technology as a force multiplier — it multiplies what you already are.

If you want to make better use of your time, I recommend you begin with the approach in the article *Triple Your Personal Productivity:*

https://stevepavlina.com/blog/2005/03/triple-your-personal-productivity/

The basic idea behind the article is to first measure your current level of productivity (the article explains how to do this via time logging), measure your current "efficiency ratio," and then gradually ramp it up.

I first wrote that article in 2000, and I've continually come back to this method again and again, at least once every six months. It makes me consciously aware of exactly how I use my time. I last applied it a few months ago, tracking my time usage over a period of several days, and I was surprised to find that there was little room for improvement. It took me five years since writing that article to reach this point, but I finally feel I'm using my time efficiently. I still have unproductive days now and then, but they're the exception. Most of the time I look back on my days and think, "I really got a lot done today. It would be hard to have done it any better."

Five years ago I knew what I needed to do. It took

me that long to build the strength and discipline to be able to do it on a consistent basis. *This was not easy!*

When you pursue the path of developing your personal productivity, it may cause you some days of hair-pulling and teeth-gnashing, but it does eventually pay off. I think many people are attracted to the idea of becoming more productive out of basic common sense. It doesn't take much brainpower to figure out that if you use your time more efficiently, you'll complete more tasks, and therefore you'll accumulate results faster. Personal productivity allows you to create enough space in your life to do all the things you feel you should be doing: eat healthy, exercise, work hard, deepen relationships, have a wonderful social life, and make a difference. Otherwise, something has to give. Without a high level of personal productivity, you'll likely have to give up something that's important to you. You have conflicts between health and work, work and family, family and friends. Industry can give you the ability to enjoy all of these things, so you don't have to choose work over family or vice versa. You can have both.

Of course industry is only one tool among many. It will allow you to complete your work efficiently, but it won't tell you what work to do in the first place. Industry is a low level tool. Working hard doesn't necessarily mean working smart. But this weakness of industry doesn't remove its powerful place in your personal development toolbox. Once you've decided on a course of action and see your plans laid out in front of you, nothing can do the job as well as industry. In the long run your results will come from your actions, and industry is all about action.

Chapter 6

Persistence

Nothing in the world can take the place of Persistence. Talent will not; nothing is more common than unsuccessful men with talent. Genius will not; unrewarded genius is almost a proverb. Education will not; the world is full of educated derelicts. Persistence and determination alone are omnipotent. The slogan "Press On" has solved and always will solve the problems of the human race.

Calvin Coolidge

Persistence is the fifth and final pillar of self-discipline.

What Is Persistence?

Persistence is the ability to maintain action regardless of your feelings. You press on even when you feel like quitting.

When you work on any big goal, your motivation will wax and wane like waves hitting the shore. Sometimes you'll feel motivated; sometimes you won't. But it's not your motivation that will produce results — it's your action. Persistence allows you to keep taking action even when you don't feel motivated to do so, and therefore you keep accumulating results.

Persistence will ultimately provide its own motivation. If you simply keep taking action, you'll eventually get results, and results can be very motivating. For example, you may become a lot more enthusiastic about dieting and exercising once you've lost those first 10 pounds and feel your clothes fitting more loosely.

When to Give Up

Should you always persist and never give up? Certainly not. Sometimes giving up is clearly the best option.

Have you ever heard of a company called Traf-O-Data? What about Microsoft? Both companies were started by Bill Gates and Paul Allen. Traf-O-Data was the first company they started, back in 1972. You can read the story of Traf-O-Data here:

https://en.wikipedia.org/wiki/Traf-O-Data

Gates and Allen ran it for several years before throwing in the towel. They gave up. Of course they did a little better with Microsoft.

If they hadn't given up on Traf-O-Data, then we wouldn't have such rich collections of Microsoft and Bill Gates jokes today.

So how do you know when to press on vs. when to give up?

Is your plan still correct? If not, update the plan. Is your goal still correct? If not, update or abandon your goal. There's no honor in clinging to a goal that no longer inspires you. Persistence is not stubbornness.

This was a particularly difficult lesson for me to learn.

Persistence

I had always believed one should never give up, that once you set a goal, you should hang on to the bitter end. The captain goes down with the ship and all that. If I ever failed to finish a project I started, I'd feel very guilty about it.

Eventually I figured out that this is just nonsense.

If you're growing at all as a human being, then you're going to be a different person each year than you were the previous year. And if you consciously pursue personal development, then the changes will often be dramatic and rapid. You can't guarantee that the goals you set today will still be ones you'll want to achieve a year from now.

My first business was Dexterity Software. I started it in 1994, fresh out of college. But after running it for more than a decade, I was ready for something new. I still run Dexterity on the side, but it's not my full-time focus anymore. It takes me only about an hour or two a week to maintain it, partly because I designed it to be as automated as possible and to provide me with a passive income. It was successful to the extent I wanted it to be. I could have continued to grow it much larger, but I knew I didn't want to spend the rest of my life making computer games. Creating my own game company was my dream at age 22, and after publishing a couple dozen games, I feel I accomplished that goal. 22-year old Steve is very satisfied. But today I have different dreams.

Did I give up on Dexterity? You could say that, but it would be more accurate to say that I was infected by a new vision of something that was far more important to me. Had I stubbornly persisted with Dexterity, this site would never have existed. I'd be working on a new game instead of my first book.

In order to make room for new goals, we have to delete or complete old ones. And sometimes new goals are so compelling and inspiring that there's no time to complete old ones — they have to be abandoned half-finished. I've always found it uncomfortable to do this, but I know it's necessary. The hard part is consciously deciding to delete an old project, knowing it will never be finished. I have a file full of game ideas and some prototypes for new games that will never see the light of day. Consciously deciding that those projects had to be abandoned was really hard for me. It took me a long time to come to grips with it. But it was necessary for my own growth to be able to do this.

I still had to solve the problem of setting goals that might become obsolete in a year due to my own personal growth. How did I solve this problem? I cheated.

I figured out the only way I could set long-term goals that would stick would be if they were aligned with my own process of growth. The pursuit of personal growth has long been a stable constant for me, even though it's paradoxically in flux at the same time. So instead of trying to set fixed goals as I did with my games business, I began setting broader more dynamic goals that were aligned with my own growth. This new business allows me to pursue my personal growth full-out and to share what I learn with others. So growth itself is the goal, both for myself and others. This creates a symbiotic relationship, whereby helping others feeds back into my own growth, which in turn generates new ideas for helping others. Anyone who's been reading this site since last year has probably seen that effect in action.

The direct and conscious pursuit of personal growth is the only type of mission that would work for me. If I made it my mission to master real estate investing, for example, I'd probably become bored with it after a few years. Since I want to keep growing indefinitely, I have to maintain a certain level of challenge and keep raising the bar ever higher. I can't let things get too dull and risk falling into a pattern of complacency.

The value of persistence comes not from stubbornly clinging to the past. It comes from a vision of the future that's so compelling you would give almost anything to make it real. The vision I have of my future now is far greater than the one I had for Dexterity. To be able to help people grow and to solve their most difficult problems is far more inspiring to me than entertaining people. These values started oozing out of me as I ran Dexterity because I favored logic puzzle games that challenged people to think, often passing up the opportunity to publish games I felt would make money but which wouldn't provide much real value to people.

Persistence of action comes from persistence of vision. When you're super-clear about what you want in such a way that your vision doesn't change much, you'll be more consistent — and persistent — in your actions. And that consistency of action will produce consistency of results.

Can you identify a part of your life where you've demonstrated a pattern of long-term persistence? I think if you can identify such an area, it may provide a clue to your mission — something you can work towards where passion and self-discipline function synergistically. I wish you great success in your efforts.

www.ingramcontent.com/pod-product-compliance
Lightning Source LLC
Chambersburg PA
CBHW061300040426
42444CB00010B/2439